Setting
Boundaries

Veronica Ray

Hazelden
Publishing

About Hazelden Publishing

As part of the Hazelden Betty Ford Foundation, Hazelden Publishing offers both cutting-edge educational resources and inspirational books. Our print and digital works help guide individuals in treatment and recovery, and their loved ones. Professionals who work to prevent and treat addiction also turn to Hazelden Publishing for evidence-based curricula, digital content solutions, and videos for use in schools, treatment programs, correctional programs, and electronic health records systems. We also offer training for implementation of our curricula.

Through published and digital works, Hazelden Publishing extends the reach of healing and hope to individuals, families, and communities affected by addiction and related issues.

For more information about
Hazelden publications,
please call **800-328-9000**
or visit us online at
hazelden.org/bookstore

INTRODUCTION

*Codependents need boundaries. We need
to set limits on what we shall do to and
for people. We need to set limits on what
we will allow people to do to and for us.
The people we relate to need to know we
have boundaries.*

—Melody Beattie
Codependent No More

Setting boundaries begins our recovery
from the effects of our relationships with
addicted, compulsive, or abusive people.
As Melody Beattie wrote, we need to set
limits on what we'll give to others and what
we'll take from them. We need to let others
know where our boundaries are and that
we are serious about them. Then, we need
to change our behavior accordingly, back-
ing ourselves up with positive action.

By setting clear boundaries on our behavior and what we will accept from others,
we begin to take back our lives from being
controlled by other people's thoughts, feelings, and problems. We claim ownership
of and responsibility for ourselves.

Setting limits doesn't mean intolerance or selfishness. It means refusing to allow ourselves to be harmed. It means accepting responsibility for our own beliefs, feelings, and actions. It means learning how to take care of ourselves, one day at a time.

Choices

Feeling compelled to control or react to others is part of codependency. Recovery means discovering all our other options. We don't have to let others and their problems and addictions control us. We have choices.

Recognizing that we do have choices is the beginning of freeing ourselves from codependency. Taking responsibility for those choices and making them requires vigilance. In many situations, old compulsive habits will probably surface first. But we can choose not to act on them, and instead turn our attention to our other options.

We have the ability, the right, and the responsibility to choose how we will think, feel, and act in every case. And, with our Higher Power's help, we can make the best choices for us.

I will not allow my feelings, thoughts, or actions to be dictated by others.

Taking a Break

In the middle of conversations, arguments, or even thoughts about our relationships, we often can't see things clearly. We can be so influenced by others that we become confused about what *we* think and how *we* feel.

It can help us to stop talking, yelling, or thinking about a conflict we have with someone else for a while. We can let go for a few minutes and clear our minds. Just leaving the room for a moment can often help us to regain our focus. We can take a walk, say a prayer, or just close our eyes and go to that place in our thoughts where we feel calm, serene, and whole.

Melody Beattie wrote in *Codependent No More*, "There is little in our lives we need to do that we cannot do better if we are peaceful." Take a moment to get peaceful.

I will honor myself by taking a break from others when I need to.

Relationships

Relationships have an important place in our lives. We interact with family members, friends, co-workers, employers or employees, neighbors, clients, and others every day.

Sometimes these relationships take up most of our time and energy. We lose our focus on work, other interests, and personal growth. We develop codependent behaviors such as caretaking, controlling, obsessing, denial, and dependency.

We can learn to have relationships without letting them control our thoughts, behaviors, and choices. Healthy relationships don't take over our lives and stop our growth. They enhance our lives and provide opportunities for us to learn and teach. They don't determine who we are; they help us discover our true selves.

I can keep myself focused on my own growth and well-being.

Balance

A good, healthy relationship includes balancing time alone and time together, dependence and independence, giving and receiving, saying yes and saying no.

This doesn't mean that everything is carefully divided down the middle. We don't keep score of hours spent together, or the number of times we give and receive favors, or the ways in which we are dependent and independent. But imbalance in these areas may make us feel discomfort that signals our need to find a better balance.

Balance is giving generously, knowing there is plenty for us too. It's receiving without guilt, and saying yes because we know we can also say no. It's trust that the relationship isn't harmed by time apart or differences of opinion. It's enjoying the low tide, secure in the knowledge that the high tide will come again.

I maintain balance in my relationships, trusting their constant ebb and flow.

Taking Risks

When we begin taking care of ourselves, many areas of our lives may change. Old relationships may be altered or ended. New relationships may be formed. Long-standing patterns of behavior may no longer fit into our lives. Letting go of old habits can feel as though we're risking our safety and comfort.

But when we go ahead and make the changes we need to for our well-being and growth, we find the risks are well worth taking. Only when we risk losing some of our old ways of living can we open up to new, better ones.

Trusting our Higher Power, we can let go of our dependence on others and find ourselves. We can stop letting ourselves be hurt and discover the alternative isn't worse, but much better. With our Higher Power's guidance, taking risks is far safer than standing still.

I ask my Higher Power for guidance and courage to take the risks I need to take.

Responsibility

To behave and live responsibly, we need to understand we are each responsible for our decisions, thoughts, attitudes, and actions. We are responsible for our recovery from defective character traits and destructive behavior.

As codependents, we may have taken on responsibilities outside ourselves. We may have "helped" others by covering up for them and removing the consequences of their negative behavior. We may have fulfilled their obligations or tried to control and manipulate their lives. We may have neglected our own responsibilities while we focused on other people's.

But others are responsible for themselves, as we are for ourselves. This means that we need to let go of other people's responsibilities and concentrate on our own.

I am fully responsible for myself, and let others take responsibility for themselves.

Pleasing Ourselves

As codependents, we often spend a lot of our time and energy trying to please others. But we may feel uncomfortable or guilty doing things for ourselves. We may expect other people to take responsibility for our happiness. We may feel we're missing out on the pleasurable side of life.

We can learn to please ourselves, making our lives more enjoyable. We can *do unto ourselves as we would have others do unto us.* In other words, we can treat ourselves as we would like to be treated.

We can give ourselves gifts, like a long walk or a hot bath. We can listen to music we like, let the phone ring and not answer it, or cook our favorite meal. We can take ourselves out for a birthday celebration or buy ourselves flowers.

Learning to please ourselves doesn't make us selfish, it helps to make us sane.

Today I will spend time and energy on myself.

Saying No

We all want to be liked and accepted by others. We want to be thought of as dependable and responsible. We want to belong, to feel wanted and needed.

But for codependents, this can become a self-destructive compulsion. We try to fulfill every request made of us. We try to stretch our time and energy to meet the needs and desires of everyone except ourselves. We say yes when we want to say no.

Saying no may be a new experience for us, requiring some practice. We can start slowly, with little things. We can learn to stop a moment and think about whether we really want to do something before we say yes. We can let go of feeling responsible for everything and guilty for sometimes saying no. We can remember our right and responsibility to take care of ourselves.

Today I will not say yes when I want to say no.

Self-Image

Where does the image we have of ourselves come from? Has it been created by what others think we are or want us to be? Is it based on comparisons with other people? Does it change depending on who is with us?

Today we can choose to let our inner voice and our Higher Power tell us who we are. No matter where we are or who we're with, we can make a conscious effort to retain our healthy, whole self-image. We don't suddenly become children because our parents are in the room. We aren't incompetent failures at life because someone successful and happy walks by. The presence of someone who once hurt us with unkind words needn't trigger self-hate in us. We can remember that we are the only ones who can choose our self-image.

I choose to see my highest, best self, with my Higher Power's help.

Drawing Lines

As codependents, we may have felt we'd reached the limit of our ability to accept another's behavior toward us. We may have declared, "This is the last time!" Then, when the next time came along, we rationalized, excused, ignored, and accepted it again. We may have done this over and over in a relationship.

It is our responsibility to take care of ourselves and do what's necessary for our well-being. That may mean setting some limits in relationships and sticking to them. It may mean changing our old habits of reaction to another's behavior. It may mean leaving a relationship.

In a calm state of mind, perhaps with a counselor or spiritual advisor, we can determine reasonable limits of acceptable behavior. Then, we can back ourselves up with whatever action is necessary to support our decision.

It is my right and responsibility to take care of myself.

Space Between Us

In a healthy relationship, we accept that each of us has unique thoughts, feelings, interests, and viewpoints. We don't feel threatened by differences, because we trust, respect, and honor each other. Our relationship doesn't depend on giving up ourselves.

We may share many activities, interests, and beliefs. We may agree on many issues and decisions. But we are also free to disagree, to pursue separate interests, and to keep growing and changing in our unique ways. Our personal growth contributes to the deepening and strengthening of the relationship.

Joining together is a beautiful human experience when it is shared by two whole people, complete in themselves. The space between us is not a pit of lions, ready to devour us. It is a free-flowing river, over which we can build a bridge of trust, respect, and love.

I lovingly accept the space between us. I am whole and complete by myself.

Standing Up

We may sometimes feel like the victims of others. They ignore us, mistreat us, take us for granted, and always expect us to help them. They forget our birthdays, our plans, and our phone numbers when they're going to be late.

How can they do this to us? The answer is that they can't—at least not without our cooperation. If we feel someone is treating us like a doormat, there can be only one solution: to get up off the floor.

Standing up for ourselves may be a new experience for many of us. With practice, we can learn to say no, to refuse to take on others' problems, to begin taking care of ourselves. We can stop being conspirators in our own abuse.

I will stand up for myself and stop being a victim.

Seeking Approval

Everyone wants the approval of others. But as codependents, we may allow our lives to be controlled by our efforts to gain this approval. We may give away all our choices, opinions, likes, and dislikes to others. We may allow our thoughts and feelings to be dictated by others, losing touch with our true selves.

We may go along with whatever others around us are saying or doing, or allow ourselves to be bullied or coerced. Whenever we let other people choose for us, we are hurting ourselves. The approval we get is never truly satisfying when we have given away ourselves to get it.

Our Higher Power guides us to our unique purpose in life when we listen to His voice. We don't need anyone else's approval. God shows His approval through our peace of mind.

Today I will let God be my only guiding force. No one can control my thoughts or actions.

Who Am I?

In order to set boundaries between ourselves and others, we need to think about who we are—and who we are *not*. A problem we have spent tremendous amounts of time and energy worrying about may not even be *our* problem at all. We may have focused so much attention on others that we have ignored ourselves. But each of us must walk our particular path alone.

To learn who we are, we turn our attention away from the obsessive thoughts that haunt our minds. We focus instead on listening for the voice of our Higher Power. Through prayer and meditation we can let God help us stop identifying with other people and their problems. Then we can face our own lives and responsibilities fully. We can discover who we are by detaching from who we clearly are not.

Letting go and letting God take care of others frees me to follow my path.

Decision-Making

As we set boundaries between ourselves and others, we develop new ways of making decisions. Without others' opinions and wishes to influence us, we develop our decision-making ability.

At first, we may feel confused or unable to make choices. We fear making a mistake. But everyone makes mistakes sometimes, and that's all right. We can learn from our mistakes and grow better and better at making good decisions.

Often the decisions we agonize over aren't really important. Does it actually matter what we cook for dinner? What difference does it make which coat we select, or whether or not we go to a party? Many choices just don't matter that much or may be reversed later.

Learning to make decisions means listening to our inner thoughts and intuitions, making the best decisions we can, and letting go of the result.

I am learning to make my own decisions.

Dependency

When we feel close to someone, we may believe we need them for our happiness. We fear losing them because we think our well-being depends on the relationship.

Our fearfulness can make us behave in ways we believe will ensure keeping the other person with us. We may focus all our attention on pleasing them. We may give up our own opinions, choices, desires, and needs. We may panic whenever we are apart from this person.

We may confuse this kind of dependency with love. We may even believe this desperate need is proof of love. But healthy, mature love does not make us less than we are individually. Mature love enhances who and what we already are.

Our happiness can never come from another person. It comes from taking care of ourselves, accepting reality, and letting ourselves grow.

I let go of my dependency on others and find happiness within myself.

Reality Check

Sometimes we slip into old familiar behaviors without realizing it. Some old habits take over when we're not paying attention. Even old beliefs we've given up may come back before we know it.

To guard against these slips, we need to often check our thinking. In any situation, we can ask ourselves whether we're behaving out of old habits or new understanding. We can take a *reality check*—searching our thoughts, words, and behavior for delusions and false beliefs.

Establishing boundaries requires a clear perception of ourselves and others. We need to let go of our clouded images and be realistic. We know we can't control others, but does our behavior reflect this knowledge? We know we are separate individuals, but do we feel threatened by another's choices? A reality check can bring us back to the truth in any situation.

I regularly check my thoughts and behaviors against reality.

Sharing Responsibility

In close, long-term relationships, we sometimes divide responsibilities. For example, our partner may choose our political opinions or take care of finances while we assume responsibility for our social life and choice of friends.

This arrangement may seem simple, but what happens when one of us doesn't like a choice the other has made? What do we do if a decision the other usually handles has to be made on the spot, and the other person isn't available?

Some choices, such as our opinions and feelings, should never be given away. Other responsibilities, like calling a plumber or shopping for food, can be shared or traded off with our partner so we both remain capable of handling them.

I can be close to another person without losing myself.

Caring or Caretaking?

We want people we love to be happy, healthy, and successful. We avoid harming them and respect their uniqueness.

Caretaking, on the other hand, is obsessive and controlling. We don't just wish others well, we try to make it happen for them. We worry, manipulate, advise, and monitor. We take over their responsibilities.

The difference between caring and caretaking is detachment. When we care about someone, we hope they are happy, but we know their happiness isn't our responsibility. We want them to grow, but understand that only they can make that happen. We accept that they are separate individuals, with their own thoughts, desires, needs, and point of view.

We can love others without taking over their lives and trying to solve their problems. We can care without caretaking.

I let go of others' problems, needs, desires, and choices.

Possessiveness

No one can ever possess another person, but we may feel as if we do. We may feel we have a right to control someone because we love them. We may believe that, if they love us, they should spend all their time with us and give up other friends and interests.

Possessiveness means we don't accept the other person's individuality. Out of fear of abandonment and mistrust of others, we're threatened by their other relationships or interests. We don't believe they'll come back to us after we've been apart, or we think they'll find someone they like better if they look around.

We can let go of our possessiveness when we accept responsibility for our own well-being. We will find that we are whole and complete in ourselves, ready to love others without needing to possess them.

I let go of possessiveness. Others belong to themselves, just as I belong to me.

Centering

Where is the center of our world? Does everything we do revolve around someone else's problems or addictions?

We choose where to place the center of our world. If we choose a center outside ourselves, we can't act for our own well-being. When we are centered in our deep, inner spiritual core, all our actions enhance our well-being.

Being centered does not mean being *self*-centered, ruled by our ego's whims, desires, fears, and distorted views. To be self-centered covers up self-hatred. Being centered reveals true self-love.

When we are centered we are focused on our Higher Power and our highest spiritual self. We are mindful of our true nature, and don't allow our decisions to be determined by others or by our egos.

My world is centered on my highest spiritual self.

Side by Side

In our relationships, we often lead others by caretaking or controlling them, or we follow others in dependency and fearfulness. We turn away from those who have hurt us, or gaze into the eyes of those we love, losing sight of everything else.

In healthy relationships, we neither lead nor follow. We walk side by side. We hold hands loosely, neither pulling nor being pulled, able to let go for a while when it's appropriate.

If our paths lead in different directions, we let the other go with our best wishes. We don't try to tug them onto our path or jump over to theirs. We trust and respect our partner.

Side by side, we can both see clearly ahead, choosing each step we take, knowing the other is nearby to love and share.

I don't need to lead or follow in my relationships.

Self-Direction

Codependent behavior includes reacting, usually quickly and inappropriately, to everything and everyone around us. We don't take time to think about what's happening and calmly decide on the best thing to do.

We can be self-directed, rather than controlled by everything outside us. This does not mean letting self-will take over. It means we don't allow other people's feelings and problems to determine our own. It means taking time to examine what's really going on and figuring out how to take care of ourselves. Before we do or say anything, we find serenity and peacefulness and call upon our Higher Power for help.

By taking the time to think clearly, we can see where our best interests lie. With our Higher Power's help, we can find our inner direction and stop being blown about like a weather vane.

I will take the time I need to be self-directed.

Irresponsibility

We may grow resentful if we take on more than our share of responsibility. Feeling tired, taken for granted, we may recognize our over-responsibility and decide to stop carrying everyone else's load. But not understanding what rightfully belongs to others, we may drop everything, including those things for which we are truly responsible.

Going from one extreme to the other won't help us. It is irresponsible to neglect our children, work, or financial obligations, or to disregard others' feelings and rights. It is irresponsible to neglect our own health and well-being.

We can find a balance between over-responsibility and irresponsibility, and take care of ourselves without taking on others' problems. And we can always find the help we need in our Higher Power.

I accept my responsibilities and let go of others'.

Assertiveness

If we allow others to control our feelings and actions, we forget how to assert ourselves. Assertiveness is not aggression or acting out anger or hostility or selfish disregard for others. Being assertive means knowing our rights as human beings.

We have a right to fun and good feelings. We have a right to say no. We have a right to grow and change. We have a right to feel and express our feelings in a nondestructive way. We have a right to make mistakes and a right to disagree. We have a right to leave the company of anyone who harms us in any way. We have a right to sanity and peace.

No one else is responsible for our personal rights. It is up to us to stand up for ourselves.

I am responsible for asserting myself.

Wholeness

We've probably heard someone's spouse referred to as "my other half," or "my better half." We often call a couple "Johnandsusan," as if it were one name, or "The Clarks," even when talking about one of them. We may say, "They owe me money," when only John borrowed from us. Or we may assume if one is Republican, a football fan, or vegetarian, both are.

We may consider these to be innocent labels and assumptions, but they can create and reinforce images of ourselves as less than whole. Our perceptions and self-image may be based on our being half of a relationship rather than being our unique selves.

Remembering our wholeness as separate individuals will help us avoid dependency in our relationships. Our health, happiness, and spirituality depend on no one but ourselves.

I am whole and complete.

Choosing Our Feelings

Sometimes, when we feel worried, sad, or angry, it may be hard to believe that we are actually choosing to feel that way. It may seem that others created those feelings in us.

But we can choose to detach ourselves from other people's feelings and behaviors. When we understand that their thoughts, feelings, decisions, and actions are not ours, we can make room for our own. We can listen without involving ourselves in another's problems. We can learn to act rather than react.

When we detach, all our feelings will come from our true inner selves, not from responses to everything outside of us. It's okay to feel anger or sadness sometimes, if they are *our* feelings. But we can also allow ourselves to feel love, forgiveness, peace, and serenity by learning to detach.

I let go of others' feelings and choose my own.

Pain

If we had to design the world, could we think of a better way to get people to stop destructive behavior than to make it painful? What could more clearly signal the need for change?

And yet, pain is often ignored, its message unheeded. It is sometimes misinterpreted or even unrecognized. But pain is not meaningless, and it will return until we hear its message.

Earnie Larsen has said, "Pain is telling us that something is wrong, that we need to behave differently, that what hurts must be fixed." Sometimes we try to change or fix the wrong things. Sometimes we leave one painful situation and head straight into another one. This is because we didn't learn the lesson within the pain.

If we pay attention to our pain, it can lead us to self-improvement, growth, and happiness.

I am open to the lessons my pain can teach me.

Selfhood

Discovering our selfhood is not just asking ourselves who we are, but also *what* we are. We often define ourselves by what we look like or what we do. But this does not answer the question of what we *are*.

Beneath the descriptions we give our bodies and personalities, lies our true identity. It is beyond being male or female, tall or short, young or old, black or white. It is at the very core of our being.

Some call it *spirit* or *soul*, others call it *love* or *creative energy*. Whatever we call it, it is our essence. It is the self we deny and ignore while we're busy operating only on the surface. But it never goes away.

Focusing on our inner selves, our spiritual development, helps us know what to do with our outer selves. Our bodies and personalities become tools for expressing our highest selves.

My spiritual center is my true self.

Changes and Endings

As we learn to take care of ourselves, our relationships are affected. Some may change a little or a lot; others may end.

These changes and endings may frighten us. Even relationships that have clearly been harmful may seem comfortable because they are so familiar. We may imagine the unknown world outside our old behaviors and relationships as threatening and dangerous, not believing we're capable of coping successfully with new relationships and experiences.

But time and persistence teach us that the changes and endings are improving our lives. We learn we can cope with life in new, healthier ways and discover abilities and talents we never knew we had. We can have relationships that enrich our lives and encourage growth.

Whatever changes we make to take care of ourselves will take us closer to health, happiness, and well-being.

The changes and endings I make will be for my highest good.

Another title that will interest you...

Codepdent No More
by Melody Beattie

The definitive book about codependency, *Codependent No More* is for everyone who has suffered the torment of loving too much. Melody Beattie explains what codependency is, what it isn't, who's got it, and how to move beyond it. This book will be a boon to your self-esteem.

208 pp.
Order No. 5014

For more information about
Hazelden publications,
please call **800-328-9000**
or visit us online at
hazelden.org/bookstore